ANATOMIES

by

J T Merry

Illustrations by James Merry

Theophrastus translations by Arthur F. Hort

Set in Doves Type Pro

Published by Abrasax Books
978-0-9573883-0-7

www.jtmerry.com

for alison, tom, alex & kate

E

CONTENTS

ANATOMIES

ῥίζα καυλὸς ἀκρεμὼν κλάδος, εἰς ἃ διέλοιτ᾽ ἄν τις
ὥσπερ εἰς μέλη, καθάπερ ἐπὶ τῶν ζῴων. ἕκαστόν τε
γὰρ ἀνόμοιον καὶ ἐξ ἁπάντων τούτων τὰ ὅλα.

root, stem, branch, twig; these are the parts into which we
might divide the plant, regarding them as members,
corresponding to the members of animals: for each of these is
distinct in character from the rest, and together they make
up the whole.

Theophrastus, *Enquiry Into Plants* I.i.9

I

every april, it seems

we remember where we planted hearts
bulb-deep in soil's flesh - tentative until

earth heard our nervousness unfurl
from two chestfuls of breathlessness.

it murmured a shudder up knuckles
like cool new leaves finding light -

so suddenly touchable that night,
first the breath's stem and then came

his kiss - a flower unfolding its blue
firmly into the corners of my mouth.

II

magnolia, moon and you
    all many-petalled

had been here before. burying bones
beneath the bed you came in stems
to shed your white nightly.

magnolia, moon and you
    did wane fragrant

above my head you forced feelers
bud-first towards touch, disrupted
a whole ocean of blood
hiding silence somewhere edgeless
inside red.

magnolia, moon and you
    i swear

according to your size and phase
my full heart's tide
obediently obeys.

III

there is a rhythm to most things
but

at night, when soil-sighed flowers
shut

and the soft possibility of you falls
almost

in the gaps swelled between each
breath,

even sleepless trees see that this would
never

have worked - that when i open, you
close.

there is one common flow, a rhythm.
there is

one common breath - and then there's
you.

ὅτι μὲν οὖν κοινὴ πᾶσιν ἡ διὰ του σπρματος γένεις φανερόν. εἰ δ᾽ ἀμφοτέρως ἔνια, καὶ αὐτόματα καὶ ἐκ σπέρματος, οὐδὲν ἄτοπον, ὥσπερ καὶ ζῷά τινα καὶ ἐξ ἄλλων καὶ ἐκ της γης.

now it is evident that generation through the seed is common to all; and if some are generated in both ways, spontaneously as well as by seed, there is no absurdity: so some animals similarly come from two sources, both from other animals and from the earth.

Theophrastus, *De Causis Plantarum* I.ii.15

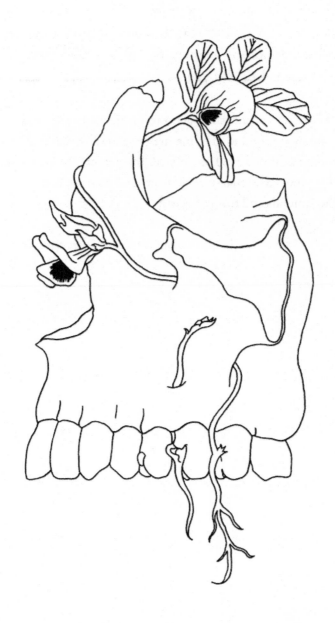

IV

in our garden even now
flowers remember their former selves
nostalgically from dirt

and fruit once bruised by our
fingernail spades still claim
the spaces where we played.

an entire childhood is in seeds
sown cthonic, deep like teeth.
witnessed only by trees, they
mark us with their own map:

under lilac, fig, beneath elderflower, inside beech
between yew and plum, walnut, on cherry's stump

all our memories are still there,
stored together as safe as beans
growing pearl-like in the gums
of their thousand silken pods.

V

in the restaurant earlier that night, it had all seemed quite hopeful. the conversation (and cutlery too) were pointing towards a set of after-dinner explorations down his arms and up his legs, which made successive shots of sake blush themselves hot between my gums.

so, i ate sideways all night – biting forwards, eyeballs glancing right - tightened his profile's line: a thread now finely veined across my retina's increasingly blurred-out backdrop. ordered some more water to swallow down what suddenly struck me as the impossibility of desire – of how anyone could ever fit those two imperfect circles perfectly on top of each other.

in the windowsill, two daffodil bulbs were trying to untie themselves skywards - likewise, my eyes watching him touched stamens against his face, and sight was suddenly a petal sensation, slightly felt right at the end of vision's stem. here i was, thinking. unravelling them. i couldn't help but pick this one - this narcissus, admiring himself to death in the backs of my eyes.

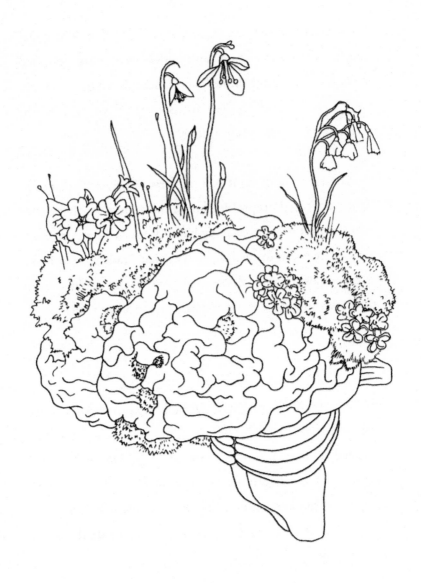

VI

these hands once held the weight of thunder
in two damp palmfuls of lead - a whole sky
compressed into a threat - held it right there
one rumbling inch, wet above your chest.

hot beneath my knees, your head then
could easily have been a dropped rock
lost, looking up from far below its own
bashed-out brains of moss.

even now, these hands can still
summon stormclouds
bruised dark with knuckles of rain.

they bury their water upwards
away from my thoughts of you.

they persuade fingers below earth
to quietly calcify into roots.

they cry themselves slowly white
in reverse, up towards your neck.

Κλείδημος δὲ σθνεστάναι μὲν ἐκ τῶν αὐτῶν τοῖς ζώοις, ὅσῳ δὲ θολερωτέρων καὶ ψυχροτέρων τοσοῦτον ἀπέχειν τοῦ ζῷα εἶναι.

Kleidemos maintains that plants are made of the same elements as animals, but that they fall short of being animals in proportion as their composition is less pure and as they are colder.

Theophrastus, *Enquiry Into Plants* III.i.3

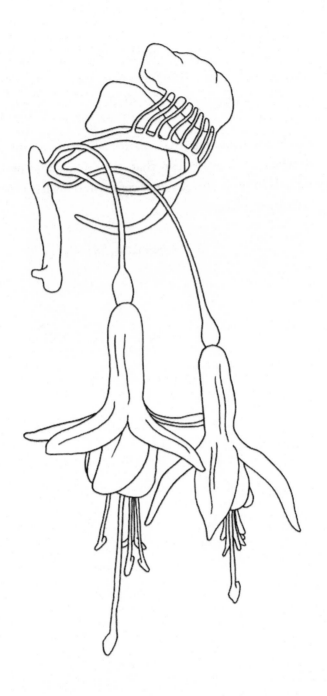

VII

this boy was slim - looked like
he'd been wearing his own skin
one size too small, all tight

nice, at first, i guess.

i said:
everything lost can be felt again in flowers.
and then i showed him:

circled his neck with a daisy chain wept.
tried, failed, then cried whole vines entire
to garland his forgetful head in leaves.

sadness can sometimes be seen
in a solid flowered form, like
two try-hard tears transforming -
almost two fuschias always falling
out of purple towards pink.

VIII

place your fears inside me

i will nurture them. your words
i would warm belly-black like eggs
forming to absorb your awkwardness.
all your stories i'd rehearse into stones
stored furtive right inside stomach's
mouth, an open hole alive now - still
wide enough to swallow hands down
with all those things we never said
digesting

out there, in that darkness
desire like flies devoured
lines up, always dissolving.

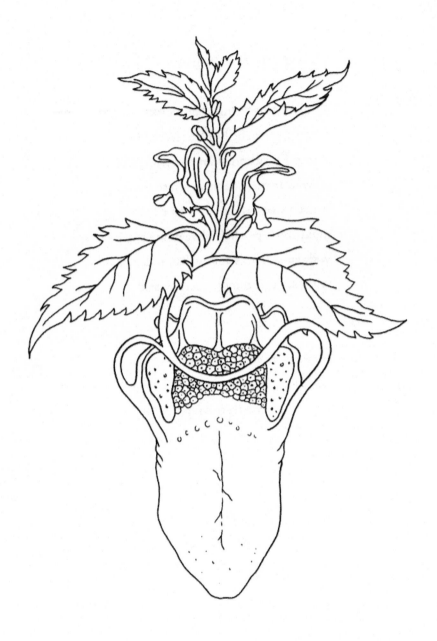

IX

if touch could somehow turn all
suddenly furred into a sort of taste
then yes

i'd let him sting my fingertips wet
with a full hand's lick around
that waist.

if mouths could forget their edges
i would. i'd let every edge lose again
against his.

all sensations overlap - with him
every sense folds so entirely inside
the next

that while you're doing it to him
it almost feels like you're doing it
to yourself.

τὰ δὲ σπέρματα πάντων ἔχει τινὰ τροφὴν ἐν αὑτοῖς, ἢ συναποτίκτεται τῇ ἀρχῇ καθάπερ ἐν τοῖς ᾠοῖς· ἢ καὶ οὐ κακῶς Ἐμπεδοκλῆς εἴρηκεν φάσκων " ᾠοτοκεῖν μακρὰ δένδρεα," παραπλησία γὰρ τῶν σπερμάτων ἡ φύσις τοῖς ᾠοῖς.

The seeds of all contain within themselves a certain amount of food, which is brought forth together with the starting point, as in eggs. Thus Empedocles has not put it badly when he says: "the tall trees lay their eggs".

Theophrastus, De Causis Plantarum I.vii.1

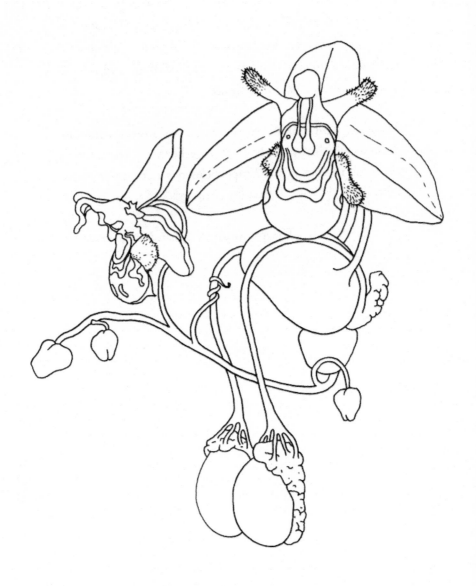

X

my bedsheets keep these silent maps
remembering only
        white

where

at some point during the night
your body had become a bud
      bed-warm

open sepal wide

to me
behaving the way an orchid must
always adapt itself towards the bee:

re-shaping every cell from inside perpetually

to find the only form which might provide
total desire: solidified.

XI

beneath the earth in tubes, dirt's darkly thirst
has urged desire through soil between our heads
and from those worm-warm stores of water burst
full stems to wake thought's seedlings from their bed.
these shoots are hungry like salt. and they yearn
to force full hands through walls of starch inside,
drawn blindly down in dark - compelled to turn
by auxin's parched portent - their only guide.
this constant urge for a fluid filtration
is really just the osmosis of lust:
when hearts are lured from a low concentration
to zones far richer in a residual trust.

       so if around your feet new fears might grow
       old roots will show: as above, so below.

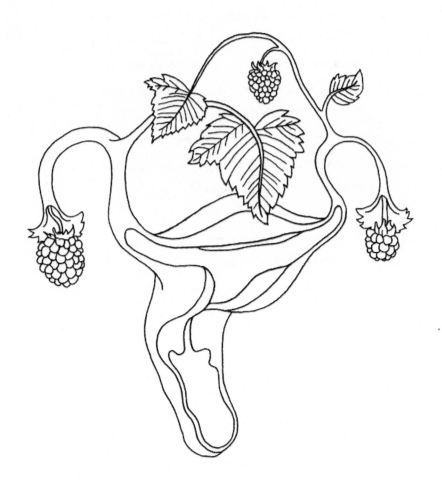

XII

even a root, which must surely know
most things about growth
could offer no detailed explanation for
the precise hows of human caprification.

how
an entire sky inside her could catch alight, how
air could ever unpick its liquid edges to find
such a sudden centre, spinning those waters so
finally forward towards form.

if you wanted to know how she guessed
where and when to condense in segments
it would be foolish to expect an answer
from a root

because liquid's residual instruction for shape
is a secret lost - suggested only by other fruit.

ἔχουσι γὰρ ὥσπερ ἶνας· ὅ ἐστι συνεχὲς καὶ σχιστὸν καὶ ἐπίμηκες, ἀπαράβλαστον δὲ καὶ ἄβλαστον. ἔτι δὲ φλέβας.

Thus plants have what corresponds to muscle; and this quasi-muscle is continuous, fissile, long: moreover no other growth starts from it either branching from the side or in continuation of it. Again, plants have veins too.

Theophrastus, *Enquiry Into Plants* I.ii.6

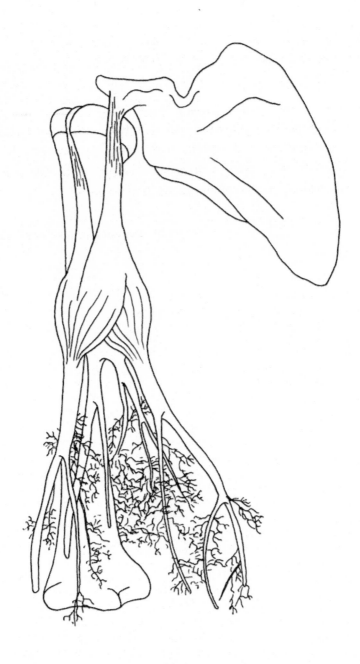

XIII

symmetry
has built a sometimes secret him
inbetween things:

between days distancing texts, spacing
the slit between his two front teeth, it
silences the gaps between cd tracks -
that's where i built him.

it fills the skin tissue-quick, this him.
exists only in the gaps between.
it tells us what theophrastus knew:
that even plants have muscles too.

inbetween everything else i hid his
real shape, unknown. held it there
below my tongue — only showed it once when asked:

what gives a gap its exact shape in space — i'd say:

it's him.

XIV

it is awkward like autumn,
nervousness.

in rooms full of people, just speaking
might try for flowers and fall wiltingly.

it embarrasses its own hedge-face red
suddenly fresh with a freckling of berries.

nervousness
grows ice inside a second spine, feels
like salt kissing snow, first it dries

then finds its way into a glass branch
dendritic to the tips of juddering knees.

nervousness
will watch itself trying trembles to end
the endings of everyone else's sentences

when actually

one berry would make a much better full-stop
decisive right there at the conversation's end.

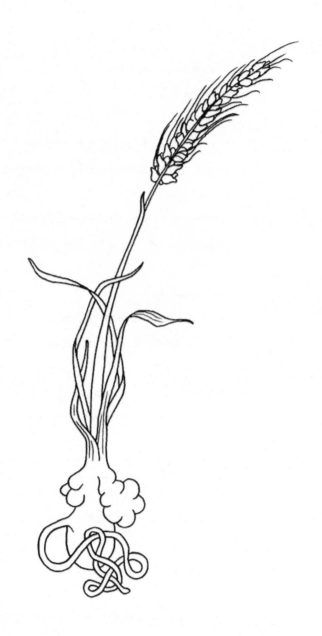

XV

we were moon-watching on the lawn when i finally took control - rolled the telescope's focus tight like a toothpaste's final squeeze, since the moon did dollop bright mint in our palms. down here, our bare feet in the dark grass were washed orange in the streetlamp's rinse. peering over the wall it watched us talk amongst those fat blades, their colding hair all on stalks

when

a mention of daylight in the sheets on the line made his arms and mine suddenly aware that their sides hadn't brushed, that legs hadn't met trouserless yet beneath heads still not rubbing their stubbled sides alight - the whole night now self-aware, measuring sensation between our two bodies full-folliced like fields of wheat - reaped into their clustered bundles of touch. if only i had known from the start

that

when the moon did finally look the other way, our orbits were always going to overlap, and i would get close enough, at last
                                    to kiss the crop circles
                                        in his beard.

Πρῶτα δέ ἐστι τὸ ὑγρὸν καὶ θερμόν· ἅπαν γὰρ
φυτὸν ἔχει τινὰ ὑγρότητα καὶ θερμότητα σύμφυτον
ὥσπερ καὶ ζῷον, ὧν ὑπολειπόντων γίνεται γῆρας καὶ
φθίσις, τελείως δὲ ὑπολιπόντων θάνατος καὶ αὔανσις.

first come moisture and warmth: for every plant, like every
animal, has a certain amount of moisture and warmth
which essentially belong to it; and if these fall short - age
and decay. but it they fail altogether - death and withering
ensue.

Theophrastus, *Enquiry Into Plants* I.ii.5

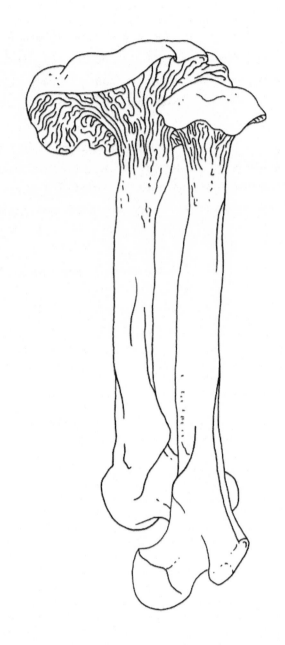

XVI

where flowers walk across a grave
the earth has found it's own slow way
to remind us that the dead can still talk
somehow, in the language of leaves

that even tears can be re-built again
in a different sort of green.

but a mushroom growing there,
lured up towards warmth from
the marrow's whispering nest

is something else

is a corpse's untold secret finally told

in a different language
never known to us;

in spores.

XVII

sleep has its own heat

rising from beneath can cause
all fleshy stores below thought
to bolt in the black: a dream is
a flare sent up, a flower nightly
 spiking air lest festering left might
sour its own water's hoard.

waking up, you could almost
catch a slim glimpse of it there

all sleep arranged in leaves, serrated white.
a dream suspended above the bed, hanging
where the light should be, and then:

a creature sat square upon my chest.
a cathedral carved in one second of salt.
a dream: dissolved.

XVIII

if standing up is just a balancing act
unfolding

then every small movement towards you
might distribute dust. rubbed inside water
like some sort of smoke, it sends my head
the instructions for dizziness – while you

nearby, still unbalance all thought into birds
sent screaming from their never-there trees.

ἐπεὶ καὶ ἐν τοῖς ζώοις τὰ μὲν συνεκτίκτεται τὰ δ᾽ ἀποκαθαίρεται καθάπερ ἀλλότρια τῆς φύσεως. ἔοικε δὲ παραπλησίως καὶ τὰ περὶ τὴν βλάστησιν ἔχειν.

even in animals there are things which are separated from the parent when the young is born, and there are other things which are cleansed away, as though neither of these belonged to the animal's essential nature. So too it appears to be with the growth of plants.

Theophrastus, *Enquiry Into Plants* I.i.3

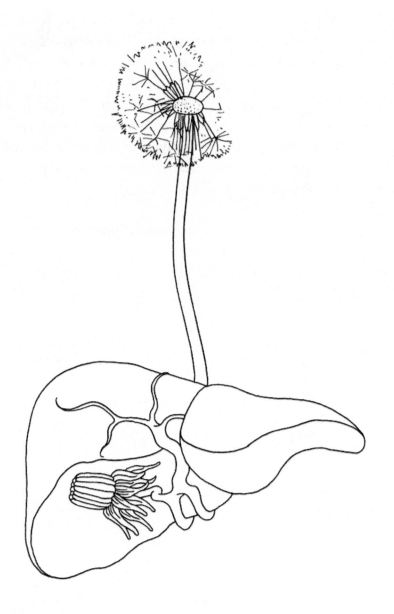

XIX

letting go

might be easier   if
a heart cut in half
(like a liver in quarters)
could re-think itself

anew too.

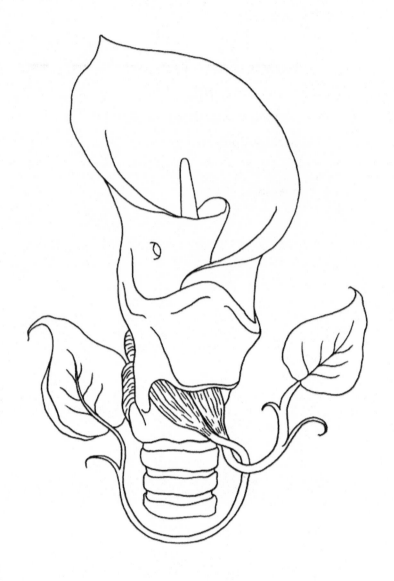

XX

sound, maybe
might show you how she grows

unbuttoning her buds - she's just
a flower in fast-forward too,
those noisy petals defining the room.

a wildflower at root - she is
throat-grown. from inside out
it's hers - it belongs to her alone.
and just to show you she'd grow;

she'd send a melody in two tendrils
coiled, then stretch from a hum's bud
all the way up to a full mouth's bloom

and then, only when her fingers decide

she'd take herself and everything else
all of a sudden back to bud.

XXI

death is easy, descends
much quicker than sleep

can even empty a spleen far faster
than a poppy might fill with milk
then bend every stem, trying in vain
to persuade the red out of white.

remembrance, however, is made to wait.
must first grow a new set of heavy heads
confronting death with a full face of seeds.
a poppy might remind us that, in the end

blood will always forget red
then remember istelf green instead
     perennially
touchable again.

ταύτῃ μὲν οὖν δόξειεν ἂν μερίζεσθαι τὸ τῆς αὐξήσεως.

all this, then, would make it appear that growth is carried on by taking turns.

Theophrastus, De Causus Plantarum I.xii.4